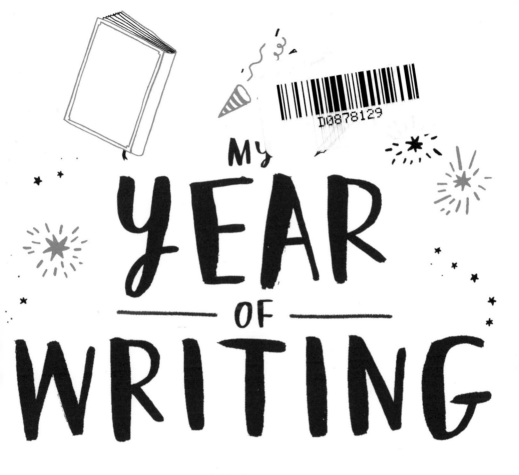

MY YEAR OF WRITING

ANNE ROONEY

ILLUSTRATED BY CHARLOTTE FARMER

THIS BOOK BELONGS TO

Kane Miller

A DIVISION OF EDC PUBLISHING

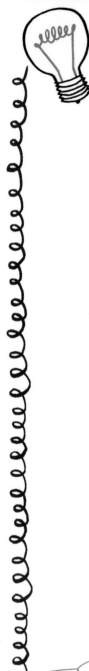

HELLO, WRITER!

This book is your very own journal for you to practice and perfect your writing. The most important thing a writer can do is to **WRITE**—every day, if possible.

Inside, there are 365 writing challenges. That's one for **EVERY DAY OF THE YEAR.** They cover all kinds of writing, including stories, poems, persuasive writing, and the nitty-gritty of different tricks and techniques. Some will only take a minute, while others might take much longer. You can complete the challenges in any order—just pick one that appeals to you and get started!

JUST REMEMBER:

1. **BE BOLD**—this is a space to explore ideas and try new things. Let your imagination run wild!

2. Know that there are **NO** wrong answers or bad ideas.

3. Have fun! **ENJOY** writing and playing with words.

4. Once you're done, you'll have a **ONE-OF-A-KIND** record of your year.

ANNE ROONEY

BEFORE YOU GET STARTED ...

You won't need many materials to do your writing; just a pen or pencil is enough. But writers often use other useful tools that you might like to try, such as:

· a dictionary: helps you check the exact meaning and spelling of words
· a thesaurus: lists other words with the same or similar meaning to the one you look up
· a computer: you can write on the computer and print your work out to glue into the book if you prefer.

OFF THE PAGE

If you're worried about changing your mind, or if you want more space to write, you can write or type on another piece of paper and glue it into the book.

DON'T STRESS

Remember, it doesn't matter if you struggle to spell, or have dyslexia. This journal is not about grades or getting things perfect—it's about your ideas, so just go with it!

HANDY DEFINITIONS

NOUN: A word that refers to a person, place, or thing.

VERB: A word in a sentence that shows action, or tells you what something is doing.

ADJECTIVE: A word that describes a noun.

1.

WHAT DO YOU SUPPOSE WHALES TALK ABOUT? FILL IN THE SPEECH BUBBLES.

2.

WHAT IS YOUR FAVORITE COLOR?
LIST AS MANY SHADES OF THAT COLOR AS YOU CAN THINK OF.

3.

WRITE ABOUT SOMETHING YOU LOST. DESCRIBE IT. HOW DID YOU FEEL ABOUT LOSING IT?

4.

WOULD YOU RATHER BE A SOCK OR A GLOVE? WHY?

5.

YOU'RE A DOG AT THE ANIMAL SHELTER; WRITE AN AD FOR YOURSELF. WHAT ARE YOU LOOKING FOR IN A FAMILY? WHAT ARE YOU LIKE?

6.

YOU'RE THE CAPTAIN OF A PIRATE SHIP. DESCRIBE YOUR CREW. LIST THEIR NAMES AND SOMETHING INTERESTING ABOUT EACH OF THEM.

7.

GIVE THIS HAT A MAGICAL ABILITY. WHAT DOES IT DO TO THE WEARER? WRITE YOUR ANSWER ON THE LINE BELOW.

8.

WRITE ABOUT SOMETHING THAT MAKES YOU FEEL PEACEFUL.

9.

WRITE A DESCRIPTION OF YOURSELF—BUT DON'T USE THE LETTER "E."

_____

_____

_____

_____

_____

_____

_____

_____

_____

10.

MAKE UP A NEW WORD. WHAT DOES IT MEAN?

11.

YOU'RE STRANDED ON A DESERT ISLAND. YOU HAVE THREE ITEMS WITH YOU. WHAT ARE THEY?

1. _____

_____

2. _____

_____

3. _____

_____

12.

WOULD YOU RATHER BE ABLE
TO BREATHE UNDERWATER
OR FLY? WHY?

13.

WHAT QUALITIES DO YOU
THINK A GOOD LEADER NEEDS?
LIST THEM HERE.

_____

_____

_____

_____

_____

_____

_____

_____

14.

A SIMILE COMPARES ONE THING WITH ANOTHER, SUCH AS
"ICE SPARKLING LIKE DIAMONDS." FINISH THESE SIMILES:

CLOUDS AS FLUFFY AS... _____

_____

_____

FALLING LEAVES CLUSTERING LIKE... _____

_____

_____

A NIGHT AS DARK AS... _____

_____

_____

15.

YOU SEE A GREEN LIGHT STREAK ACROSS THE SKY AND THEN A SHOWER OF SPARKS A SMALL DISTANCE AWAY. WHAT DO YOU FIND WHEN YOU GET CLOSER?

_____

_____

_____

_____

_____

_____

_____

_____

16.

IF YOU COULD HAVE ANY HAIRSTYLE YOU WANTED, WHAT WOULD IT BE LIKE?

17.

DESCRIBE YOUR PERFECT HOME. IT COULD BE A CASTLE, A NEST, AN IGLOO, A TENT—OR ANYTHING ELSE.

18.

WHAT'S YOUR FAVORITE ANIMAL?
WRITE A DESCRIPTION FOR THE WILDLIFE PARK.

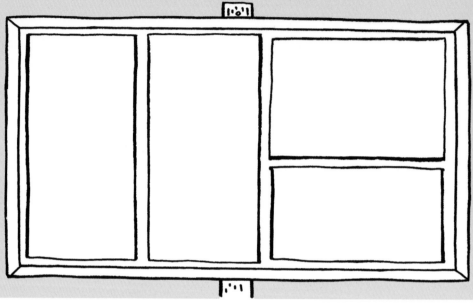

19.

WRITE THE LONGEST
WORD YOU KNOW.

20.

YOU VISIT A SPOOKY HOUSE
AND FIND AN OLD DESK.
YOU OPEN A SECRET
DRAWER AND THERE ARE
THREE THINGS IN IT.
WHAT ARE THEY?

1. _____

2. _____

3. _____

21.

THINK OF SOMEONE YOU KNOW WELL. WHICH THREE WORDS DESCRIBE THEM BEST?

1. _____

2. _____

3. _____

22.

WHAT WOULD IT BE LIKE TO LIVE IN A CAVE?

23.

MAKE UP A NEW SNACK, CANDY, OR CAKE, AND WRITE AN AD FOR IT.

24.

IF YOU COULD HAVE ANY
CHARACTER FROM A STORY AS YOUR
TEACHER, WHO WOULD IT BE? WHAT
SUBJECT WOULD THEY TEACH?

25.

WRITE DOWN AS MANY FOODS
AS YOU CAN THINK OF THAT
START WITH THE LETTER "B."

26.

YOU GO TO THROW SOMETHING
IN A DUMPSTER AND FIND A
POLKA-DOT SUITCASE IN IT.
WHAT'S INSIDE THE SUITCASE?

27.

WHAT IS YOUR FAVORITE
TYPE OF WEATHER? WHAT
DO YOU ENJOY MOST
ABOUT IT?

28.

WHAT'S THE STORY BEHIND THIS PICTURE?

_____

_____

_____

_____

_____

_____

_____

_____

_____

_____

_____

_____

_____

_____

29.

REWRITE A FAIRY TALE OR FOLKTALE USING ONLY 50 WORDS. THIS KIND OF WRITING IS CALLED "FLASH FICTION."

_____

_____

_____

_____

_____

_____

_____

_____

_____

_____

_____

_____

_____

_____

_____

_____

_____

_____

_____

30.

WRITE DOWN AS MANY WORDS AS YOU CAN THINK OF THAT MEAN "LARGE."

31.

PRETEND YOU'RE ON A TRIP IN A SUBMARINE.
WHAT CAN YOU SEE FROM THE WINDOW?

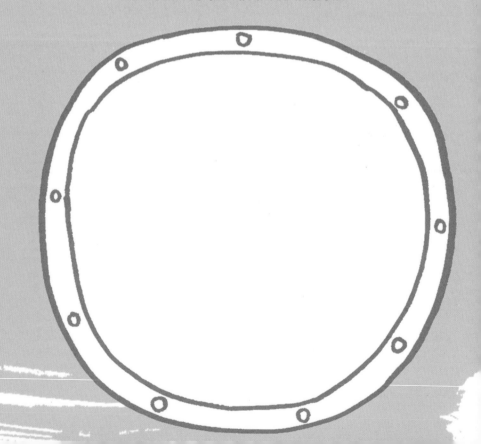

32.

INVENT A CHARACTER WITH UNEXPECTED CHARACTERISTICS—
LIKE A COWARDLY OGRE OR A KINDLY WOLF.

33.

DESCRIBE THE NEAREST PIECE OF FURNITURE TO YOU.
GIVE AS MUCH DETAIL AS YOU CAN.

34.

WHAT IF HUMANS HAD TAILS?
WHAT WOULD YOU DO WITH YOURS? WHAT WOULD IT LOOK LIKE?

35. A MOTTO IS A PHRASE THAT SUMS UP YOUR PERSONALITY AND ALSO MOTIVATES YOU, SUCH AS "SEIZE THE DAY." WRITE YOUR OWN MOTTO.

36. "DON'T GO INTO THE WOODS!"—WHY NOT?

_____

_____

_____

_____

_____

37. DESCRIBE YOUR PERFECT PICNIC. WHAT WOULD YOU EAT? WHERE WOULD YOU GO? WITH WHOM?

38.

WRITE A LETTER TO AN ADVICE COLUMN ABOUT SOMETHING THAT TROUBLES OR WORRIES YOU.

_____
_____
_____
_____
_____
_____
_____
_____
_____
_____
_____
_____
_____
_____
_____
_____
_____
_____
_____

39.

WRITE AN ANSWER TO YOUR LETTER FROM ACTIVITY 38, AS THOUGH YOU WROTE THE ADVICE COLUMN.

_____
_____
_____
_____
_____
_____
_____
_____
_____
_____
_____
_____
_____
_____
_____
_____
_____
_____
_____

40.

SOMEONE GAVE YOU THIS PRESENT.
DESCRIBE HOW YOU FEEL BEFORE YOU OPEN IT.

_____

_____

_____

_____

_____

_____

_____

_____

41.

THINK ABOUT YOUR LEAST-FAVORITE
SEASON. THEN WRITE THREE GOOD
THINGS ABOUT IT.

1. _____

_____

2. _____

_____

3. _____

_____

42.

WRITE DOWN A PROMISE THAT YOU
MADE. DID YOU KEEP IT?

_____

_____

_____

_____

_____

_____

_____

_____

43.

WHAT IS YOUR FAVORITE WORD?
WHY IS IT YOUR FAVORITE?

44.

FINISH THIS SIGN.

BEWARE

45.

LIST AN ANIMAL FOR EVERY LETTER OF THE ALPHABET.
ARE THERE ANY YOU CAN'T DO?

A _____   J _____   S _____
B _____   K _____   T _____
C _____   L _____   U _____
D _____   M _____   V _____
E _____   N _____   W _____
F _____   O _____   X _____
G _____   P _____   Y _____
H _____   Q _____   Z _____
I _____   R _____

46.

MAKE UP FIVE TOTALLY WACKY ICE CREAM FLAVORS.

1. _____
2. _____
3. _____
4. _____
5. _____

47.

A CLICHÉ IS A SAYING THAT HAS BEEN SO OVERUSED IT HAS LITTLE IMPACT, SUCH AS "TIME FLIES" OR "A BED OF ROSES." LIST AS MANY CLICHÉS AS YOU CAN THINK OF.

48.

WRITE ABOUT A TIME WHEN YOU HAD TO MAKE A CHOICE. DID YOU MAKE THE RIGHT ONE?

49.
WHAT WOULD IT BE LIKE IF YOU SHRANK TO JUST TWO INCHES TALL?

50.

YOU CAN'T BE SURE YOUR SOCKS STAY IN THE
DRAWER WHEN IT'S CLOSED. WHERE MIGHT THEY GO?

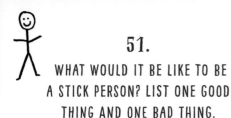

51.

WHAT WOULD IT BE LIKE TO BE
A STICK PERSON? LIST ONE GOOD
THING AND ONE BAD THING.

52.

DESCRIBE YOUR IDEAL BIRTHDAY CAKE.
WHAT DOES IT LOOK LIKE?
HOW DOES IT TASTE?

53.

WRITE A STORY BY FILLING IN THE GAPS:

WHEN... _____

_____ BUT... _____

AS SOON AS... _____

BECAUSE... _____

_____ UNTIL... _____

FINALLY... _____

54.

YOU ARE BURYING A TIME CAPSULE TO SHOW PEOPLE IN THE FUTURE
WHAT LIFE WAS LIKE IN THE 2020s. WHAT FIVE THINGS DO YOU PUT IN IT?

1. _____

2. _____

3. _____

4. _____

5. _____

55.

WRITE A REVIEW OF A BOOK YOU HAVE JUST READ. WHAT WAS
GOOD (AND BAD) ABOUT IT? WOULD YOU RECOMMEND IT?

56. YOU ARE A LEAF ABOUT TO FALL OFF A TREE. WRITE A FAREWELL OR THANK YOU NOTE TO THE TREE.

57.

WRITE A WORD (AS MANY TIMES AS YOU NEED TO) SO THAT IT ILLUSTRATES ITSELF. FOR EXAMPLE, YOU COULD WRITE THE WORD "STRING" OVER AND OVER IN A LINE UNTIL IT LOOKS LIKE A PIECE OF STRING.

58.
IF YOU WERE KING OR QUEEN, WHAT KIND OF THRONE WOULD YOU HAVE?

59.
YOU VISIT A FRIEND FOR A CELEBRATION. THEY PERFORM A VERY STRANGE WELCOMING RITUAL WHEN YOU ARRIVE. DESCRIBE IT.

60.
WRITE WHAT HAPPENS AFTER THE END OF YOUR FAVORITE MOVIE OR STORY.

61.

CONTINUE THIS STORY: "JOSEF WALKED DOWN THE BUS TO HIS USUAL SEAT, BUT IT WAS ALREADY OCCUPIED—BY A CROCODILE ..."

_____

_____

_____

_____

_____

_____

_____

_____

62.

REWRITE THIS SENTENCE USING COMPLETELY DIFFERENT WORDS FOR ALL THOSE UNDERLINED:

A <u>BROWN</u> <u>STICK</u> <u>FELL</u> FROM THE <u>TREE</u> IN THE <u>WIND.</u>

63.

WHAT WOULD THE BEST SHOES IN THE WORLD BE LIKE?

64.

YOU FALL ASLEEP ON THE
COUCH AND WAKE UP IN 2051.
WHAT IS THE WORLD LIKE?

65.

WRITE AN IDEA FOR A
NEW EPISODE OF YOUR FAVORITE
TV SHOW OR CARTOON.

66.

WOULD YOU RATHER FLY A PLANE, SAIL A SHIP, OR PILOT A SUBMARINE? WHY?

67.

WRITE ABOUT AN OBJECT WITHOUT USING ITS NAME. DESCRIBE HOW IT LOOKS AND TALK ABOUT WHAT IT IS USED FOR.

68.

WHAT WAS THE LAST THING THAT MADE YOU LAUGH? WRITE ABOUT IT.

69.

IF YOU COULD GIVE SOMEONE ELSE A MAGICAL POWER, WHOM WOULD YOU GIVE IT TO AND WHAT WOULD IT BE?

70.

MAKE UP A WORD FOR A FEELING YOU HAVE AND EXPLAIN WHAT IT MEANS.

71. A HAIKU IS A POEM THAT IS THREE LINES LONG WITH FIVE SYLLABLES IN THE FIRST LINE, SEVEN IN THE SECOND LINE, AND FIVE IN THE THIRD LINE. READ THE EXAMPLE HAIKU, THEN WRITE YOUR OWN.

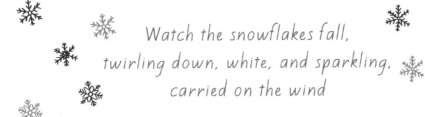

Watch the snowflakes fall,
twirling down, white, and sparkling,
carried on the wind

72.

WRITE AN INVITATION TO A PARTY YOU WOULD LIKE TO HAVE.
DON'T FORGET TO SAY WHERE AND WHEN IT IS, AND WHAT WILL HAPPEN.

73.

IMAGINE YOU HAD A TOTALLY SQUISHY BODY LIKE A SQUID, AND YOU COULD
SQUEEZE THROUGH TINY GAPS. WHERE WOULD YOU GO? WHAT WOULD YOU SEE?

74.

WRITE DOWN THREE WORDS THAT SOUND LIKE THEIR MEANING, SUCH AS "HICCUP" OR "WHISPER." THIS IS CALLED "ONOMATOPOEIA."

1. _____

2. _____

3. _____

75.

WRITE SOME RULES FOR PEOPLE VISITING YOUR BEDROOM.

76.

YOU'RE AT THE STARTING LINE, ABOUT TO RUN IN A RACE. SHOW HOW YOU ARE FEELING BY DESCRIBING YOUR PHYSICAL REACTIONS AND MOVEMENTS. FOR INSTANCE, IS YOUR HEART RACING? ARE YOU STANDING STILL?

77.

YOU ARE ABOUT TO BE EATEN BY A DRAGON!
HOW WILL YOU PERSUADE IT NOT TO EAT YOU?

78.

IT'S A HOT DAY, SO YOU GO SWIMMING AT THE LOCAL POOL. THEN YOU NOTICE THAT THE SWIMMER NEXT TO YOU HAS WEBBED GREEN FEET! WHAT IS GOING ON?

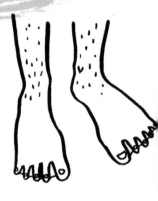

79.

YOU ARE OFFERED THE CHANCE TO
LIVE FOREVER. DO YOU TAKE IT?
EXPLAIN YOUR CHOICE.

80.

THE OWNER OF YOUR BEACHSIDE HOTEL
SAID YOU MUST NEVER FORGET
TO LEAVE A LINE OF SAND ACROSS
YOUR DOORWAY AT NIGHTTIME. WHY?

81.

YOU ARE WALKING ALONG THE BEACH AND SEE FOOTPRINTS GOING INTO A CAVE, BUT NOT OUT OF IT. DO YOU FOLLOW THE FOOTPRINTS? WHAT DO YOU FIND?

82. DESCRIBE THE KIND OF VEHICLE YOU EXPECT TO BE ABLE TO BUY WHEN YOU ARE 50 YEARS OLD.

83.

WRITE DOWN FIVE QUESTIONS YOU WOULD ASK YOUR FAVORITE FICTIONAL CHARACTER FROM A MOVIE, BOOK, OR TV SHOW.

1. _____
2. _____
3. _____
4. _____
5. _____

84.

IF YOU COULD WEAR ANYTHING TO SCHOOL, WHAT WOULD IT BE?

85.

WHAT UNUSUAL ANIMAL WOULD YOU LIKE AS A PET? IT COULD BE ANYTHING FROM A RAVEN TO A CROCODILE!

86. PRETEND THAT YOUR BODY IS MADE OF JELLO! HOW DOES IT FEEL?

_____

_____

_____

_____

_____

_____

_____

_____

_____

_____

87. MAKE UP NAMES FOR FOUR CHARACTERS IN A SPOOKY STORY,
OR A STORY SET IN THE PAST. WHAT ARE THE CHARACTERS LIKE?

1. _____

_____

2. _____

_____

3. _____

_____

4. _____

_____

88.

YOU BUY SOME SECONDHAND SNEAKERS AND DISCOVER THAT THEY GIVE YOU AN ATHLETIC SUPERPOWER. WHAT IS IT? WHAT DO YOU DO?

89.

MAKE UP A NEW FRUIT, AND GIVE IT A NAME.

90. WRITE A THANK YOU NOTE TO SOMEONE WHO SENT YOU A PRESENT.

91. WRITE AN AD FOR A VACATION ON MARS.

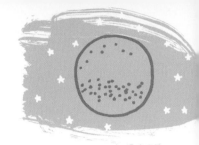

92. YOU WAKE UP AND DISCOVER THAT YOU ARE A DOG, OWNED BY YOUR FAMILY. WHAT IS YOUR FIRST DAY LIKE?

_____

_____

_____

_____

_____

_____

_____

_____

_____

93. WRITE SOME ADJECTIVES TO DESCRIBE THESE MONSTERS.

94.

EXAGGERATION FOR DRAMATIC EFFECT IS CALLED "HYPERBOLE." IF YOU'RE WAITING FOR A TRAIN, AND YOU WANT TO SHOW HOW FRUSTRATED YOU ARE, YOU MIGHT SAY, "THIS IS TAKING FOREVER!" WRITE A SENTENCE THAT USES HYPERBOLE.

95. IMAGINE YOU'RE A CELEBRITY.
HOW DID YOU BECOME FAMOUS?

96. YOU ARE LOST IN A FOREST. WHAT IS IT LIKE?

97.
YOU DEFINITELY CLOSED THE DOOR TO YOUR BEDROOM WHEN YOU LEFT. BUT WHEN YOU GET HOME, IT'S WIDE OPEN AND YOUR THINGS ARE ALL OVER THE PLACE. WHAT HAPPENED?

_____

_____

_____

_____

_____

_____

_____

_____

98.

WHY DO LEOPARDS HAVE SPOTS? GIVE A WACKY, UNEXPECTED ANSWER.

_____
_____
_____
_____
_____
_____
_____
_____
_____

99.

WHO WOULD YOU INVITE TO A DREAM PIZZA PARTY? THEY CAN BE LIVING, DEAD, OR IMAGINARY!

100.

YOU ARE WALKING HOME FROM SCHOOL AND YOU FIND A MESSAGE LYING ON THE GROUND. WHAT DOES IT SAY?

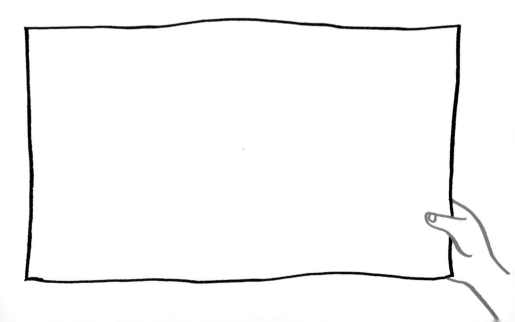

101. PRETEND YOU'RE HOLDING A VERY OLD OBJECT OF SOME KIND. DESCRIBE IT WITHOUT USING THE WORD "OLD."

102. WHICH COUNTRY WOULD YOU MOST LIKE TO VISIT? WHY?

103. YOU WAKE UP AND REALIZE YOU HAVE GROWN WINGS! DESCRIBE YOUR DAY. HOW DO YOU FEEL? WHAT DO YOU DO?

104. WRITE DOWN THE FIRST WORD YOU THINK OF WHEN
YOU SEE EACH OF THESE WORDS:

DREARY   _____

FLOODED   _____

MOUNTAIN   _____

EXHAUSTED   _____

SHY   _____

105. WRITE TWO NEW YEAR'S RESOLUTIONS
YOU WOULD LIKE TO BE ABLE TO KEEP.
THEY DON'T HAVE TO BE REALISTIC!

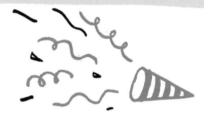

106. WHAT IF YOU WERE AN INTELLIGENT ROBOT? WHAT RIGHTS DO YOU THINK YOU SHOULD HAVE?

107.

YOU FIND A NOTE IN YOUR COAT POCKET TELLING YOU TO GO TO A PARTICULAR PLACE IN YOUR SCHOOL AT NOON TOMORROW. WHAT HAPPENS WHEN YOU GET THERE?

108.
WHAT WOULD IT BE LIKE
TO HAVE A PET GIRAFFE?

109.
WHAT WORDS COULD YOU USE
INSTEAD OF "SAID" IN A STORY?

110.
WHAT IS IT LIKE TO HAVE A LOOSE
TOOTH? EXPLAIN IT FOR SOMEONE
WHO HASN'T HAD ONE.

111. WHAT WOULD THESE VEGETABLES SAY IF THEY COULD TALK? FILL IN THE SPEECH BUBBLES.

112. WHAT WOULD IT BE LIKE TO LIVE IN THE CLOUDS?

113.
WRITE A ONE-SENTENCE DESCRIPTION OF A SWAMP OR A BOG. BE AS VIVID AS YOU CAN.

114.
THE OPPOSITE OF A WORD IS CALLED ITS "ANTONYM." FIND ANTONYMS FOR THESE WORDS:

GRUMPY _____

PARCHED _____

FRAGILE _____

SPRINGY _____

FURRY _____

115. YOU'RE AN ARCHEOLOGIST ON A DIG AND YOU DISCOVER AN ANCIENT SCROLL INSIDE A TOMB. WHAT DOES IT SAY?

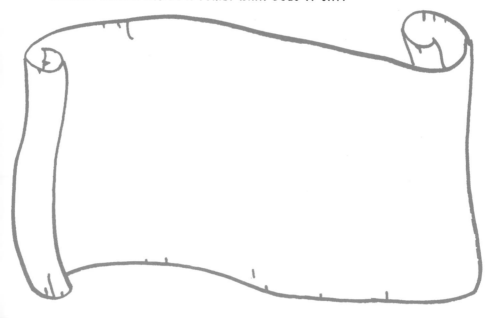

116. HOW HAS THIS MERMAID ENDED UP ON THE SUBWAY?
WRITE HER EXPLANATION IN THE SPEECH BUBBLE.

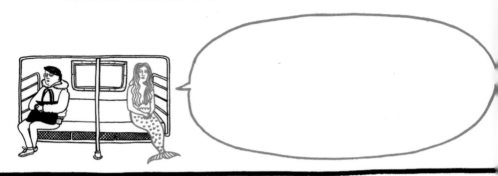

117.
LIST FIVE THINGS YOU
ARE GOOD AT.

1. _____

_____

2. _____

_____

3. _____

_____

4. _____

_____

5. _____

_____

118.
IF YOU COULD STUDY ANY SUBJECT
AT ALL—REAL OR IMAGINARY—WHAT
WOULD IT BE? WHY?

119. WRITE ABOUT THE LAST TIME YOU WERE EXCITED.

_____

_____

_____

_____

_____

_____

_____

_____

_____

_____

120. YOU FIND A KEY IN YOUR POCKET. IT'S DEFINITELY
NOT YOURS. WHAT DOES IT OPEN?

121.

WHAT'S AT THE OTHER
END OF THE STRING?

122.

WRITE ABOUT A VACATION YOU
WOULD LOVE TO GO ON.

123.

A PALINDROME IS A WORD THAT
IS SPELLED THE SAME BOTH
FORWARD AND BACKWARD, SUCH
AS "DAD" OR "NOON." CAN YOU
THINK OF ANY OTHERS?

124.

WHAT CAN YOU SEE OUTSIDE THE
NEAREST WINDOW, RIGHT NOW?

125.

NAME THIS ANIMAL AND DESCRIBE ITS BEHAVIOR, FEATURES, AND PERSONALITY.

126. YOU GET TO RENAME THE DAYS OF THE WEEK. WHAT DO YOU CALL THEM?

MONDAY————————

FRIDAY————————

TUESDAY————————

SATURDAY————————

WEDNESDAY————————

SUNDAY————————

THURSDAY————————

127. YOU'RE AN ASTRONAUT AND YOUR SPACESHIP HAS JUST BEEN SUCKED INTO A WORMHOLE! YOU END UP IN A DIFFERENT GALAXY. WHAT HAPPENS NOW?

128. IF YOU COULD FREEZE TIME FOR EVERYONE ELSE FOR ONE DAY, WHAT WOULD YOU DO DURING YOUR EXTRA DAY? REMEMBER, NO ONE ELSE CAN MOVE OR DO ANYTHING!

129.

WRITE A THANK YOU NOTE TO YOUR TEETH! WHY ARE THEY USEFUL? WHAT DO YOU LIKE ABOUT THEM?

130.

IF YOU WERE A SUPERHERO, WHAT WOULD YOUR SUPERPOWER BE? WHY?

131.

HOW WOULD YOU DESCRIBE A DOG TO AN ALIEN WHO HAS NEVER SEEN ONE?

132.

YOU ARE SITTING IN A CAFE. A GIRL AT THE NEXT TABLE ASKS YOU TO WATCH A BOX FOR A COUPLE OF MINUTES. SHE NEVER COMES BACK. THE BOX STARTS TO SHAKE AND MAKE A NOISE! WHAT HAPPENS NEXT?

133.

YOU'VE INVENTED A MACHINE
THAT WILL MAKE YOUR LIFE
EASIER. WHAT DOES IT DO?

_____

_____

_____

_____

_____

_____

_____

134.

YOU ARE ON A BOAT, GOING TO
START A NEW LIFE IN A LAND FAR
AWAY. WRITE A FAREWELL MESSAGE
TO YOUR FRIENDS BACK HOME.

135.

WHO LIVES IN
THIS TOWER?

136. DESCRIBE A PLACE YOU KNOW WELL, BUT DON'T SAY WHAT ANYTHING LOOKS LIKE. CONCENTRATE ON SOUNDS, TEXTURES, SMELLS, AND HOW THE PLACE MAKES YOU FEEL.

137. WRITE AN ANTHEM (A CELEBRATORY SONG) FOR YOUR SCHOOL.

138. WHAT'S THE KINDEST THING YOU HAVE EVER DONE FOR SOMEONE ELSE? WRITE ABOUT IT HERE.

_____

_____

_____

_____

_____

_____

_____

_____

_____

139. WHAT'S ON THIS TROLL'S SHOPPING LIST?

140. USING ONLY 10 WORDS, DESCRIBE WHAT YOU THINK IT'S LIKE TO LIVE IN A TIDE POOL.

141.

WRITE A SHORT STORY, STARTING WITH THIS SENTENCE:
"IT WAS A CLOUDLESS NIGHT WITH A BRIGHT FULL MOON—
BUT THERE WASN'T A SINGLE STAR IN THE SKY ..."

142.
YOU BUY AN OLD LAMP. WHEN YOU CLEAN IT, A GENIE APPEARS. WHAT HAPPENS NEXT?

143.
WRITE DOWN RHYMES FOR EACH OF THESE WORDS:

SPOON _____

CHAIR _____

HONEY _____

RICE _____

TREE _____

144.
WRITE DOWN ALL OF THE ADJECTIVES YOU CAN THINK OF TO DESCRIBE FOOD.

145.
IMAGINE YOU HAVE A MAGIC LUNCHBOX THAT CONTAINS WHATEVER LUNCH YOU WANT. WHAT WOULD IT CONTAIN TODAY?

146. WRITE A NOTE TO YOUR FUTURE SELF DESCRIBING ONE OF YOUR LIFE GOALS.

147. IF YOU HAD AN INVISIBILITY CLOAK, WHERE WOULD YOU WEAR IT? WHAT WOULD YOU DO?

148. WHAT IF HUMANS WERE LIKE INSECTS AND HAD SIX LIMBS? WOULD YOU PREFER TO HAVE EXTRA LEGS OR EXTRA ARMS? WHAT WOULD YOU DO WITH THEM?

150. DESCRIBE YOUR PERFECT TREEHOUSE.

149. PRETEND YOU ARE ON THIS TRAIN. WHERE IS IT GOING? WHAT IS IT LIKE? WHO IS SITTING NEXT TO YOU?

151.

YOU HAVE WON A PRIZE FOR YOUR WRITING! WHAT WILL YOU SAY IN YOUR ACCEPTANCE SPEECH?

152.

HOW MANY WORDS CAN YOU THINK OF TO DESCRIBE DIFFERENT SMELLS?

153.

IF YOU COULD BE ANY TYPE OF ANIMAL FOR A DAY, WHAT WOULD YOU BE?

154. FINISH THIS AD FOR FLYING CARPET RIDES.

155. YOU HAVE DISCOVERED A NEW PLANET! WHAT WILL YOU CALL IT?

156. FILL IN THIS DAILY SCHEDULE FOR MAGIC SCHOOL.

	9-10	10-11	11-12	LUNCH	1-2	2-3	
MONDAY							

157. WHAT IS YOUR FAVORITE MONSTER FROM A SCI-FI OR FANTASY STORY OR MOVIE? EXPLAIN WHY IT'S YOUR FAVORITE.

_____

_____

_____

_____

_____

_____

_____

_____

_____

_____

158. WRITE ABOUT SOMEONE OR SOMETHING YOU MISS.

159. MAKE AS MANY WORDS AS YOU CAN FROM THE LETTERS IN THIS WORD: "FLABBERGASTED."

160. WHAT ARE THESE SOCK PUPPETS SAYING TO EACH OTHER?

161. WRITE DOWN THE LAST DREAM YOU REMEMBER HAVING.

162. WHAT WOULD A MERMAID'S HOME BE LIKE? IMAGINE YOU'RE VISITING AND DESCRIBE WHAT YOU SEE.

_____

_____

_____

_____

_____

_____

_____

_____

163. THE ENGLISH WRITER A. A. MILNE WROTE STORIES ABOUT HIS SON'S TOYS, INCLUDING A STUFFED BEAR NAMED WINNIE-THE-POOH. WRITE A STORY ABOUT SOME OF YOUR TOYS.

_____

_____

_____

_____

_____

_____

_____

_____

164. YOU ARE A SCIENTIST AND YOU HAVE MADE A WONDERFUL DISCOVERY. WHAT IS IT? WHAT WILL YOU CALL IT? DESCRIBE IT.

165. WHAT IS YOUR FAVORITE TEACHER LIKE? WHY ARE THEY YOUR FAVORITE?

166. YIKES! YOU HAVE BEEN SWALLOWED BY A WHALE. WHAT'S IT LIKE IN THERE?

167. DESCRIBE WHAT IT WOULD BE LIKE IF YOU LIVED ON THE CEILING, UPSIDE DOWN, LIKE A FLY WITH STICKY FEET.

168. FILL IN THIS CROSSWORD GRID.

169.

EVERY FOUR YEARS, THERE ARE 29 DAYS IN FEBRUARY INSTEAD OF 28. THESE ARE LEAP YEARS. MAKE A PLAN FOR YOUR NEXT "EXTRA" DAY.

170.

WHAT DOES IT FEEL LIKE TO HAVE A COLD?

171.

YOU TAKE DOWN A POSTER AND FIND A MESSAGE WRITTEN ON THE WALL BEHIND IT. WHAT DOES IT SAY?

172. A JAPANESE LEGEND SAYS EARTHQUAKES ARE CAUSED BY A GIANT UNDERGROUND CATFISH NAMED NAMAZU WRIGGLING IN THE MUD. MAKE UP YOUR OWN EXPLANATION OF A NATURAL EVENT.

_____

_____

_____

_____

_____

_____

_____

_____

_____

_____

_____

173. GIVE A NAME TO EACH FINGER AND THUMB ON YOUR HAND.

175.

TWO WORDS THAT MEAN THE SAME THING ARE "SYNONYMS." WRITE SYNONYMS FOR EACH OF THESE WORDS.

ANXIOUS _____

VIBRANT _____

HUNGRY _____

WELL-BEHAVED _____

174.

ONE MORNING YOU GO OUTSIDE AND THERE ARE TWO SUNS IN THE SKY! WHAT HAPPENED?

176.

THINK OF A NAME FOR THIS IMAGINARY ISLAND.

177.

HOW DOES A RACEHORSE FEEL WHEN IT'S RUNNING A RACE? TRY TO IMAGINE, THEN DESCRIBE IT.

178. WRITE A VERY SHORT STORY IN WHICH A CELL PHONE IS IMPORTANT.

_____

_____

_____

_____

_____

_____

_____

_____

_____

_____

179.

LOOK AT THE EXAMPLE, THEN ADD AN ADJECTIVE IN FRONT OF EACH OF THE NOUNS.

A _fidgety_ PUPPY

A _____ SPACESHIP

A _____ CAVE

A _____ MONSTER

180.

YOU FIND A NEST ABANDONED BY A BIRD THAT LIKED TO COLLECT SHINY THINGS. DESCRIBE WHAT YOU FIND INSIDE IT.

181. THERE'S A SCHOOL PLAY AND YOU WANT TO BE IN IT. WHAT PART DO YOU WANT TO PLAY? WHY ARE YOU PERFECT FOR THE ROLE?

_____

_____

_____

_____

_____

_____

_____

_____

_____

_____

_____

_____

_____

182. WHAT IS YOUR FAVORITE KIND OF TREE? WHAT MAKES IT SPECIAL TO YOU?

183. YOU ARE ABOUT TO BLAST OFF FOR MARS. YOU WILL BE GONE FOR FIVE YEARS. WRITE A GOOD-BYE LETTER TO SOMEONE YOU LOVE.

184. PHRASES LIKE "DEAFENING SILENCE" AND "ACT NATURALLY" ARE OXYMORONS. AN OXYMORON PUTS TOGETHER TWO WORDS WITH CONFLICTING MEANINGS. WRITE DOWN AS MANY OXYMORONS AS YOU CAN THINK OF.

185. DESCRIBE, IN AS MUCH DETAIL AS YOU CAN, SOMETHING YOU ARE CURRENTLY WEARING.

---

186. WHAT IF YOU WERE A CHAIR? WOULD YOU LIKE HELPING PEOPLE REST? OR WOULD IT BE UNCOMFORTABLE TO BE SQUASHED?

---

187. IF YOU COULD MAGICALLY SHRINK ONE OBJECT SO THAT YOU COULD CARRY IT AROUND WITH YOU, AND THEN MAKE IT BIGGER AGAIN WHEN YOU WANTED TO, WHAT WOULD IT BE?

188.

IF YOU WERE A GREAT ARTIST, WHAT WOULD YOUR MASTERPIECE BE?
A PAINTING? A SCULPTURE? DESCRIBE IT.

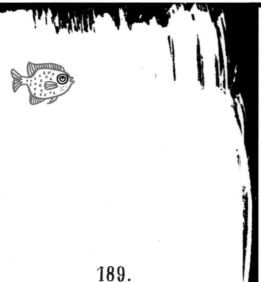

190.

WHAT DO YOU THINK
THIS MACHINE DOES?

189.

WHAT WOULD IT BE LIKE
TO BE A FISH?

191.

IF YOU COULD RELIVE ONE DAY FROM YOUR PAST, WHICH WOULD IT BE?

192.

YOU WANT TO GO TO THE BEACH,
BUT YOUR FRIEND WANTS TO GO
TO THE MOVIES. WRITE WHAT YOU
WOULD SAY TO PERSUADE THEM.

193. PRETEND YOU HAVE A PEN PAL IN ANOTHER COUNTRY. WRITE A LETTER DESCRIBING YOUR LIFE, YOUR FAMILY, YOUR SCHOOL, OR WHATEVER YOU LIKE.

_____

_____

_____

_____

_____

_____

_____

_____

194. MAKE A POEM OUT OF YOUR NAME. FIRST, WRITE YOUR NAME VERTICALLY, SO THAT EACH LETTER IS A SEPARATE LINE, THEN USE EACH LETTER TO START A NEW WORD, PHRASE, OR SENTENCE. THIS IS KNOWN AS AN "ACROSTIC" POEM.

195.
WHOSE CAPE IS THIS?
WHAT IS IT FOR?

196.
IMAGINE YOU'RE AN OGRE.
WHAT'S YOUR FAVORITE SNACK?

197.
THIS BALL HAS JUST BEEN KICKED.
WHAT IS IT SAYING?

198.
DESCRIBE THE BEST BIRTHDAY
PRESENT YOU EVER RECEIVED.

199.
THINK OF A WONDERFUL SMELL AND DESCRIBE IT AS VIVIDLY AS YOU CAN.

200.
THINK OF A WICKED CHARACTER AND IMAGINE THAT THEY HAVE AN UNEXPECTED HOBBY, LIKE ICE-SKATING OR KNITTING! WHAT'S THE HOBBY?

201.
WHAT IS THE TREASURE BURIED AT X? WHO PUT IT THERE, AND WHY?

202.

YOU GET TO SPEND A DAY ON THE MOON. WHAT DO YOU DO THERE?

203.

WHAT WOULD IT BE LIKE
IF SNOW WAS WARM?

204.

THIS SOCK IS A SUPERHERO.
GIVE IT A NAME AND A
SUPERPOWER.

205.

THINK OF THINGS OR OBJECTS THAT ARE CIRCULAR, LIKE THE MOON. WRITE DOWN AS MANY AS YOU CAN THINK OF.

206.

WHAT'S THE STORY BEHIND THIS AD?

FOR SALE

COWBOY HAT
SLIGHTLY
CHEWED

207.

YOU'RE TAKING A WALK IN AN ENCHANTED FOREST.
WHO DO YOU MEET? WHAT HAPPENS NEXT?

_____

_____

_____

_____

_____

_____

_____

_____

_____

208.

WHOSE EYES ARE THESE? WHAT
WILL THEIR OWNER DO NEXT?

209.

WRITE ABOUT YOUR LAST
DAYDREAM.

210. YOU DISCOVER A STRANGE EGG. IT STARTS TO CRACK. DESCRIBE THE CREATURE THAT COMES OUT OF THE SHELL.

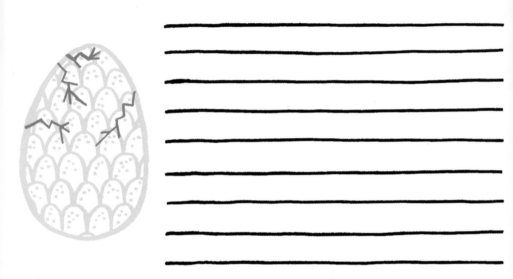

211. IF YOU OWNED YOUR OWN BUSINESS, WHAT WOULD YOU CALL IT? WHAT WOULD YOUR BUSINESS DO?

212. WHAT WOULD IT FEEL LIKE TO BE A WALRUS LYING ON AN ICE FLOE?

213. IF YOU COULD FIX ANY PROBLEM IN THE WORLD, WHAT WOULD IT BE, AND WHY?

214. IMAGINE IF THE SUN DISAPPEARED AND IT WAS DARK ALL DAY LONG. WHAT WOULD LIFE BE LIKE?

215. FOLLOW THE EXAMPLE AND SWAP THESE PHRASES FOR A SINGLE VERB.

CREEP SECRETLY   *sneak*

SHAKE WITH COLD

EAT QUICKLY

SMILE BROADLY

216. YOU'RE A POLICE OFFICER AND IT'S YOUR JOB TO INTERVIEW THE BIG BAD WOLF. WRITE DOWN THREE OF THE QUESTIONS YOU ASK.

1. _____
   _____

2. _____
   _____

3. _____
   _____

217. YOU'RE WRITING A MYSTERY STORY. DESCRIBE THE HERO AND THE VILLAIN.

218. YOU'RE GIVEN A MAGIC POTION. DO YOU DRINK IT? WHAT DOES IT DO?

219.

A MARTIAN IS COMING TO VISIT YOUR HOMETOWN. WRITE A LIST OF FUN THINGS THEY CAN DO OR SEE DURING THEIR STAY.

220.

A METAPHOR USES AN UNRELATED WORD OR PHRASE AS A WAY OF DESCRIBING SOMETHING ELSE. FOR EXAMPLE, "A BLANKET OF FOG" IS NOT A REAL BLANKET, BUT IT'S MORE VIVID THAN "A LAYER OF FOG." TRY WRITING TWO SENTENCES THAT USE METAPHORS.

221.

WRITE A "BLURB" (A SHORT DESCRIPTION) FOR THE BACK COVER OF THIS BOOK. TRY TO MAKE IT INTRIGUING WITHOUT GIVING AWAY WHAT HAPPENS.

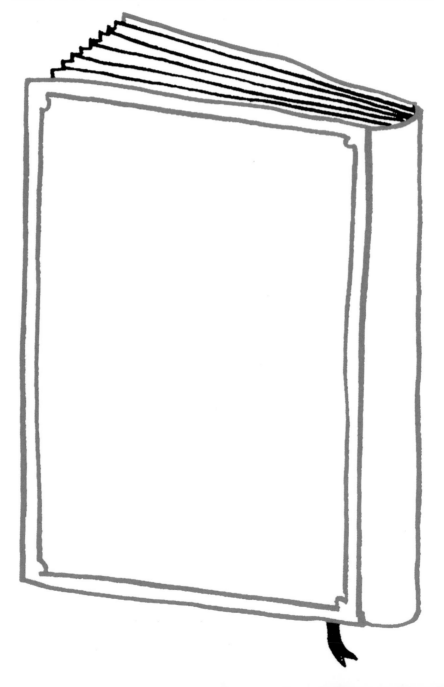

222.

WHAT IS THE WORST THING YOU HAVE TO DO NOW BUT WON'T HAVE TO DO WHEN YOU ARE A GROWN-UP?

_____

_____

_____

_____

_____

223.

ONE DAY YOU DISCOVER A SECRET DOOR IN YOUR HOUSE OR SCHOOL. WHAT HAPPENS WHEN YOU GO THROUGH IT?

224.

HOW MANY DIFFERENT WORDS CAN YOU THINK OF THAT MEAN "SMALL"? LIST THEM HERE.

225.
WRITE ABOUT A CHARACTER WHO LEAVES HOME AND TRAVELS TO ANOTHER COUNTRY. WHAT IS THEIR NEW LIFE LIKE?

KEEP OFF THE

PLEASE DO NOT CROSS THE

THE RESTROOMS ARE NOW BEING CLEANED BY A

NO

226.
COMPLETE EACH OF THESE SIGNS TO MAKE THEM MUCH MORE INTERESTING THAN USUAL.

227. WRITE ABOUT SOMETHING YOU ARE AFRAID OF. THEN WRITE HOW YOU COULD TACKLE YOUR FEAR.

---

228. LEAVE INSTRUCTIONS FOR SOMEONE WHO WILL BE TAKING CARE OF YOUR PET (REAL OR IMAGINARY) WHILE YOU ARE AWAY.

229. ONE DAY, YOU GO OUTSIDE AND THE SKY IS BRIGHT RED. WHAT HAPPENED?

230. DESCRIBE AN ANIMAL THAT MIGHT LIVE
10 MILLION YEARS IN THE FUTURE.

231.

WHAT WOULD YOUR DREAM
JOB BE AND WHY?

232.

PRETEND YOU ARE A BABY BIRD,
ABOUT TO FLY FOR THE FIRST TIME.
HOW DO YOU FEEL?

233. "JAN WAS HAVING A GREAT DAY UNTIL IT STARTED RAINING—BIG, FAT DROPS OF PURPLE RAIN. THEN ..." WRITE WHAT HAPPENS NEXT.

_____

_____

_____

_____

_____

_____

_____

_____

_____

234. PICK A STORY YOU LIKE AND WRITE A NEW ENDING.

_____

_____

_____

_____

_____

_____

_____

_____

_____

_____

235. LIST SOME THINGS THAT MAKE YOU THINK OF FALL.

236.

YOU HAVE MET A CYCLOPS!
WHAT DO YOU TALK ABOUT?

237.

WRITE DOWN FIVE THINGS
THAT MAKE YOU SMILE.

1. _____

2. _____

3. _____

4. _____

5. _____

238. WHAT DO YOU THINK THE AREA YOU LIVE IN WOULD HAVE BEEN LIKE WHEN DINOSAURS ROAMED THE EARTH?

239. DESCRIBE YOUR FAVORITE OUTFIT.

_____
_____
_____
_____
_____
_____
_____

240. IT'S TIME FOR A JOKE! IT COULD BE ONE YOU'VE HEARD BEFORE, OR ONE YOU'VE MADE UP.

241. YOU GET TO SCHOOL AND NO ONE RECOGNIZES YOU. WHAT HAPPENED?

_____

_____

_____

_____

_____

_____

_____

_____

242. IF YOU COULD LIVE ANYWHERE YOU WANTED, WHERE WOULD THAT BE?

243. PRETEND YOU'RE WRITING A STORY ABOUT SOME FIERCE VIKINGS. DESCRIBE YOUR MAIN CHARACTER.

244. WRITE A DIARY ENTRY FOR A DAY IN THE LIFE OF A HIPPOPOTAMUS.

245. YOU WAKE UP IN THE MORNING TO FIND THE TOOTH FAIRY TRAPPED UNDER YOUR PILLOW. WHAT HAPPENS NEXT?

246.

WRITE THREE THINGS YOU WOULD ADD TO YOUR NEIGHBORHOOD IF YOU COULD,
SUCH AS AN ICE CREAM PARLOR OR A SWIMMING POOL.

1. _____

2. _____

3. _____

247.

WRITE DOWN ALL THE ORANGE
THINGS YOU CAN THINK OF.

248.

WOULD YOU RATHER LIVE
IN A HOT DESERT OR ON
A SNOWY MOUNTAIN? WHY?

249.

WRITE A SMALL SHAPE POEM, LIKE A POEM ABOUT STARS
WHERE THE WORDS ARE WRITTEN IN THE SHAPE OF A STAR.

250.

IMAGINE IF YOUR TEACHER TURNED INTO A CAT! WHAT SORT OF THINGS WOULD THEY TEACH YOU?

251. WHAT LIVES IN THIS CAVE?

_____
_____
_____
_____
_____
_____
_____
_____
_____
_____

252. WRITE CLEAR, STEP-BY-STEP INSTRUCTIONS FOR BRUSHING YOUR TEETH. DON'T LEAVE ANYTHING OUT.

253. YOU FIND A SCRAP OF PAPER AT THE SUPERMARKET. IS IT A REGULAR GROCERY LIST? OR SOMETHING MORE EXCITING?

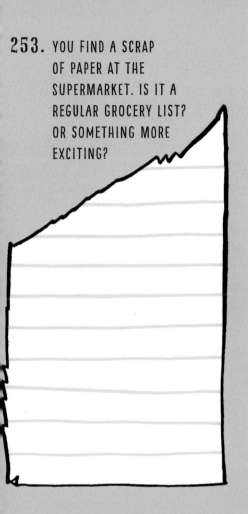

254. WHAT WOULD THE MOST SCARY INSECT IN THE WORLD BE LIKE?

255. UH-OH ... YOU UPSET A WICKED WITCH AND SHE TURNED YOU INTO A TREE! WRITE ONE GOOD THING AND ONE BAD THING ABOUT YOUR NEW LIFE.

GOOD:

BAD:

256. PRETEND YOU ARE A FEARSOME PIRATE. WHAT IS YOUR NAME?

257. YOU'RE THE PRINCIPAL OF A SCHOOL. LIST THREE SCHOOL RULES.

1. _____
   _____

2. _____
   _____

3. _____
   _____

258. IF YOU WERE ONLY ALLOWED TO KEEP ONE OF YOUR POSSESSIONS, WHAT WOULD IT BE? EXPLAIN YOUR CHOICE.

259. A PREFIX IS A GROUP OF LETTERS AT THE START OF A WORD THAT CHANGES ITS MEANING. FOR EXAMPLE, THE PREFIX "UN" MEANS "NOT"— SO "UNIMPORTANT" MEANS "NOT IMPORTANT." WRITE AS MANY WORDS AS YOU CAN THINK OF THAT BEGIN WITH THIS PREFIX.

260. ALL OF A SUDDEN YOU CAN READ EVERYONE'S THOUGHTS. WHAT DO YOU DISCOVER?

261. DESCRIBE THE ROOM YOU ARE SITTING IN. WHAT DOES IT LOOK LIKE? HOW WARM OR COLD IS IT? WHAT FURNITURE IS THERE?

_____

_____

_____

_____

_____

_____

_____

_____

_____

262. YOU SPEND A DAY AT THE MOST EXCITING SWIMMING POOL IN THE WORLD. WHAT IS IT LIKE?

_____

_____

_____

_____

_____

_____

_____

_____

263. YOUR PET HAMSTER STARTS TALKING TO YOU.
WHAT DOES IT SAY?

264.
WRITE A LIST OF BOOKS YOU MIGHT
FIND IN A DRAGON'S LIBRARY.

265.
WHERE IS THIS ROCKET GOING?
WHO IS INSIDE?

266.

A SENTENCE LIKE "WE WILL SOON ZOOM TO THE MOON" USES ASSONANCE: IT REPEATS THE SAME VOWEL SOUND. WRITE A SENTENCE USING ASSONANCE.

267.

WHAT WOULD IT BE LIKE TO CLIMB UP THIS TOWER?

268.

YOU OPEN YOUR WINDOW AND SEE AN ANT THE SIZE OF A PUPPY ON THE WINDOWSILL. WHAT HAPPENS NEXT?

269.

YOU ARE PARACHUTING FROM A PLANE. DESCRIBE HOW YOU FEEL AS YOU JUMP AND WHAT YOU SEE BELOW YOU.

_____
_____
_____
_____
_____
_____
_____
_____
_____
_____
_____
_____
_____
_____
_____

270.

CHANGE THE VERBS IN THESE SENTENCES SO THAT THE SENTENCES SAY SOMETHING ENTIRELY DIFFERENT.

HARRY ~~ATE~~
*threw*
A PINEAPPLE.

LILY RAN
_____
IN THE PLAYGROUND.

LATOYA DREW
_____
A CAR.

MISHA CUDDLED
_____
HER SISTER.

DANIEL STROKED
_____
A CAT.

271.

WRITE ABOUT SOMETHING YOU WOULD LOVE TO TRY IF YOU ONLY HAD THE CHANCE.

272.

WHERE WOULD YOU LIVE IF YOU COULD NEVER MOVE AGAIN?

273.

WHAT WAS THE FIRST THING YOU DID WHEN YOU GOT UP TODAY?

274.

YOU ARE SPENDING A NIGHT IN A LOG CABIN IN A FOREST. IS IT EXCITING OR SCARY? WHY?

275.

DESCRIBE SOMEONE WALKING IN A PARK, SO IT IS CLEAR THEY
ARE IN A HAPPY MOOD, BUT DON'T USE THE WORD "HAPPY."
WRITE ABOUT THEIR MOVEMENTS AND EXPRESSIONS.

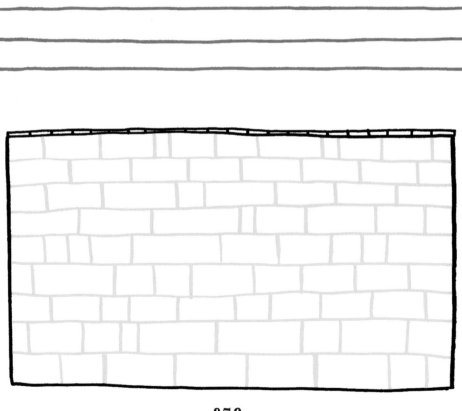

276.

WRITE SOME INTERESTING GRAFFITI ON THIS WALL.

277. THINK OF AN ANIMAL AND WRITE A SHORT POEM ABOUT IT. TRY TO MAKE THE POEM RHYME.

278. EXPLAIN SOMETHING YOU LEARNED RECENTLY. IT CAN RELATE TO SCHOOLWORK, A HOBBY, A SPORT—ANYTHING THAT INTERESTS YOU.

279. WRITE DOWN THREE QUESTIONS YOU
WOULD ASK YOUR FAVORITE CELEBRITY.

1. _____

2. _____

3. _____

280. YOU ARE DIGGING ON THE BEACH AND DISCOVER A BALL OF POLISHED
METAL. YOU PICK IT UP AND IT STARTS TO GLOW. WHAT HAPPENS NEXT?

281. YOU WANT TO BECOME A TOP SECRET SPY.
LIST SOME OF THE SKILLS YOU NEED TO HAVE.

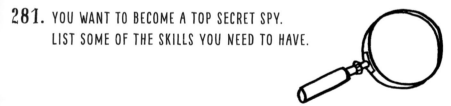

282. YOU LOOK IN THE MIRROR TO WIPE SOMETHING OFF YOUR FACE, BUT THE FACE IN THE MIRROR ISN'T YOURS! WHOSE IS IT?

283. WRITE A FEELING, SUCH AS HAPPY OR SAD, NEXT TO EACH TYPE OF WEATHER:

SUNSHINE:

RAIN:

FOG:

STORM:

284. HOW WOULD YOU DESCRIBE THE FEELING OF BEING PROUD?

285. YOU'RE MOVING TO A NEW HOUSE, BUT BEFORE YOU GO, YOU LEAVE SOMETHING HIDDEN UNDER A FLOORBOARD. WHAT IS IT?

286. IMAGINE YOU HAVE BEEN ON A SLEIGH RIDE THROUGH A SNOWY FOREST. WRITE A POSTCARD TELLING SOMEONE ABOUT IT.

287. A DISTANT RELATIVE GIVES YOU A TIME MACHINE.
WHAT TIME DO YOU TRAVEL TO? WHAT HAPPENS?

_____

_____

_____

_____

_____

_____

_____

_____

_____

_____

_____

_____

_____

_____

288. WHAT IF YOU COULD BECOME SOMEONE ELSE FOR A DAY, JUST BY
PUTTING ON THEIR CLOTHES? WHO WOULD YOU BECOME?

289. WOULD YOU LIKE TO GO DIVING WITH SHARKS? WHAT WOULD IT BE LIKE?

290. DESCRIBE THE MOST DELICIOUS MEAL YOU'VE EVER HAD.

291. "ALLITERATION" MEANS USING THE SAME SOUND AT THE START OF TWO OR MORE WORDS, SUCH AS "SUPER SOPHIE." MAKE UP THREE CHARACTERS WHOSE FULL NAMES USE ALLITERATION.

1. _____

2. _____

3. _____

292.

PREPOSITIONS ARE LINKING WORDS THAT TELL YOU HOW THINGS RELATE TO EACH OTHER. IN "THE CAT IS <u>ON</u> THE TABLE," THE "ON" TELLS YOU WHERE THE CAT IS IN RELATION TO THE TABLE. WRITE TWO SENTENCES USING PREPOSITIONS, AND UNDERLINE THE PREPOSITIONS.

293.

THINK ABOUT THE LAST TIME YOU CRIED. WHAT UPSET YOU?
HOW DID YOU FEEL?

294.

WHAT IS YOUR LEAST-FAVORITE
WORD? EXPLAIN WHY YOU DISLIKE IT.

_____
_____
_____
_____
_____
_____
_____

295.

WRITE ABOUT SOMETHING
YOU ARE GRATEFUL FOR.

296.

WHAT WOULD IT FEEL LIKE
TO BE A WORM WRIGGLING
THROUGH THE SOIL?

297.

WHAT'S IN THE BOX?

_____
_____
_____
_____
_____
_____
_____
_____

298.

WHAT FIVE WORDS WOULD
YOUR FRIENDS USE TO
DESCRIBE YOU?

299.

WHAT KIND OF FOOD DOES THIS
CREATURE LIKE TO EAT?

300.

YOU'RE A DEAP-SEA DIVER AND ONE DAY YOU DISCOVER A SECRET,
UNDERWATER CITY! DESCRIBE IT USING LOTS OF DETAIL.

301.
LIST THE BEST AND WORST THINGS ABOUT BEING YOUR AGE.

302.
YOU'RE A MOUSE. WHAT DID YOU DO THIS MORNING?

303.
YOU FIND A NOTE TAPED TO A SEAT ON THE BUS. IT SAYS, "THIS IS THE SEAT OF DOOM!" WHAT HAPPENS?

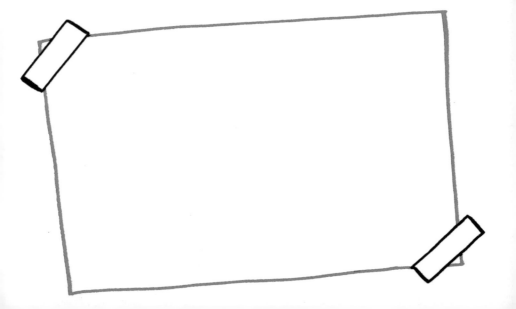

304. WRITE ABOUT YOUR FAVORITE YEARLY CELEBRATION. WHY DO YOU LOVE IT?

305. YOU'RE ABOUT TO SET OFF ON A POLAR EXPEDITION. LIST SOME OF THE EQUIPMENT YOU'LL BRING WITH YOU.

306.

MAKE A LIST OF THINGS YOU WOULDN'T BE ABLE TO DO IF SUDDENLY THERE WAS NO ELECTRICITY—EVER AGAIN!

307.

YOU ARE A STONE AGE PERSON AND YOU WANT A NEW HOME. WRITE WHAT YOU'RE LOOKING FOR IN YOUR NEXT CAVE.

308. YOU MEET A GOBLIN WHO DOESN'T KNOW WHAT LAUGHTER IS. HOW DO YOU DESCRIBE IT? WHAT COULD YOU DO TO MAKE THE GOBLIN GIGGLE?

309. WHO OWNS THESE BOOTS? HOW DID THEY END UP LOOKING LIKE THIS?

310. WRITE YOUR FULL NAME. NOW USE THE LETTERS TO INVENT A NEW NAME FOR YOURSELF.

311. DESCRIBE WHAT IT IS LIKE TO HAVE A HEADACHE.

312.

YOU WAKE UP ONE MORNING AND YOU AND YOUR MOM
HAVE SWAPPED BODIES! WHAT HAPPENS NEXT?

_____

_____

_____

_____

_____

_____

_____

_____

_____

313.

THINK OF YOUR FAVORITE CHARACTER FROM A BOOK. WHAT ARE THEIR TRAITS
OR CHARACTERISTICS, SUCH AS "BEING HONEST," OR "SECRETIVE"? LIST AS
MANY AS YOU CAN THINK OF, INCLUDING BOTH GOOD AND BAD THINGS.

_____

_____

_____

_____

_____

_____

_____

314. LOOK AT THE PICTURE AND WRITE WHAT HAPPENS NEXT.

315. MNEMONICS ARE TOOLS THAT HELP US REMEMBER THINGS. FOR INSTANCE, IF YOU STRUGGLE TO SPELL THE WORD "SAID," MEMORIZING A SILLY PHRASE THAT USES ALL THE LETTERS COULD HELP: "SNAKES AND INSECTS DANCE." MAKE UP YOUR OWN MNEMONIC TO HELP YOU REMEMBER SOMETHING.

316.

DESCRIBE AN ANIMAL, USING WORDS THAT START WITH THE SAME LETTERS AS THE ANIMAL'S NAME, LIKE "SLITHERY SLUG."

317.

WHAT HAS THE CHEF PUT IN THE STEW?

_____

_____

_____

_____

_____

318.

IF YOU COULD BE A CREATURE THAT LIVES ON A CORAL REEF, WHICH CREATURE WOULD YOU BE?

319.

SOME PEOPLE BELIEVE SUPERSTITIONS, SUCH AS, WALKING UNDER A LADDER BRINGS BAD LUCK. MAKE UP A NEW SUPERSTITION.

320. NAME THIS MONSTER— AND ITS BABIES!

321. THINK ABOUT A CONVERSATION YOU HAD YESTERDAY. WRITE DOWN AS MUCH OF IT AS YOU CAN REMEMBER.

322. YOU'RE IN A BAND. WHAT KIND OF MUSIC DO YOU PLAY? WHAT IS YOUR BAND'S NAME? WHAT IS YOUR ROLE IN THE BAND?

323. INVENT TWO CRIME-FIGHTING CHARACTERS. WHAT ARE THEIR NAMES? THINK OF THREE CLUES THEY HAVE FOUND THAT THEY CAN FOLLOW.

NAME: _____

NAME: _____

CLUE 1: _____

_____

CLUE 2: _____

_____

CLUE 3: _____

_____

324. WHEN YOU BREAK OPEN A FORTUNE COOKIE YOU FIND A PREDICTION OR SOME WORDS OF WISDOM INSIDE. MAKE UP YOUR OWN FORTUNE COOKIE MESSAGES.

325.

WHAT MADE THESE FOOTPRINTS?
WHY DID IT TURN AROUND?

326.

PICK AN OBJECT OR ANIMAL
AND DESCRIBE IT USING HUMAN
CHARACTERISTICS OR ACTIONS,
SUCH AS "DANCING LEAVES." THIS
IS CALLED "PERSONIFICATION."

_____

_____

_____

_____

_____

_____

_____

_____

327. YOU PUT YOUR HAND IN YOUR POCKET AND FEEL SOMETHING
SQUISHY, WARM, AND WET. WHAT IS IT? HOW DID IT GET THERE?

328. LIST THREE OBJECTS YOU CAN SEE AROUND YOU IN THE SECOND COLUMN. THEN WRITE AN ADJECTIVE TO DESCRIBE EACH OBJECT IN THE FIRST COLUMN.

_____	_____
_____	_____
_____	_____

329. YOUR SCHOOL BUS TAKES A DETOUR AND GOES SOMEWHERE YOU'VE NEVER BEEN BEFORE. WHAT DO YOU SEE?

330. WHAT IS YOUR BIGGEST INTEREST? IF THERE WAS A BOOK ABOUT IT, WHAT WOULD IT BE CALLED?

331. WHAT HAS HAPPENED TO THIS CASTLE?

332. WHAT KIND OF HOME DO YOU THINK THIS CREATURE LIVES IN? WHAT IS IT LIKE?

333. WRITE DOWN AS MANY WORDS AS YOU CAN THINK OF TO DESCRIBE WATER.

334. YOU TOOK A PHOTO OF YOU AND YOUR FRIEND. BUT WHO IS THAT CREATURE IN THE BACKGROUND?

_____

_____

_____

_____

_____

_____

_____

_____

335. WRITE THE OPENING PARAGRAPH OF AN EXCITING STORY. TRY TO INCLUDE THE FOLLOWING WORDS: "BANG," "MAYHEM," "FLAMINGO," "BLUE."

_____

_____

_____

_____

_____

_____

_____

_____

_____

_____

336.
THIS FAIRY GOES TO FAIRY SCHOOL. HE JUST GOT HIS REPORT CARD. LIST WHICH SUBJECTS HE IS DOING WELL IN, AND WHICH HE ISN'T.

337.
DESCRIBE A MAGICAL OBJECT THAT CAN CARRY PEOPLE TO ANOTHER WORLD. IS IT BEAUTIFUL AND ORNATE? OR SCRUFFY AND OLD?

338. THINK OF A CHORE YOU HATE DOING. NOW INVENT AN EXCUSE TO GET OUT OF DOING IT. MAKE IT AS WILD AND DRAMATIC AS YOU CAN.

339. YOU ORDER A PIZZA AND IT'S DELIVERED BY A TALL MAN WITH BLUE SKIN. YOU NOTICE HE USES A TENTACLE TO HAND THE PIZZA OVER! WHAT IS HE? AND WHY IS HE DELIVERING PIZZAS?

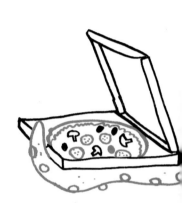

340. WRITE A SHORT GHOST STORY FROM THE POINT OF VIEW OF THE GHOST.

341.

SOME WRITERS USE A PEN NAME INSTEAD OF THEIR OWN NAME. LEMONY SNICKET, MARK TWAIN, AND DR. SEUSS ARE ALL PEN NAMES. WHAT WOULD YOURS BE?

342.

SIT OUTSIDE AND LISTEN. WRITE DOWN THE DIFFERENT SOUNDS YOU HEAR.

343.

IMAGINE HOW IT WOULD FEEL TO CHANGE FROM A CATERPILLAR TO A BUTTERFLY. DESCRIBE IT HERE.

344.

WRITERS SOMETIMES GIVE HUMAN FEELINGS TO OBJECTS OR CONDITIONS. FOR EXAMPLE, "THE WEATHER IS MISERABLE," AND "THE SAD SANDWICH WAS FORGOTTEN." THIS IS CALLED "PATHETIC FALLACY." WRITE A SENTENCE THAT USES PATHETIC FALLACY.

_____

_____

_____

_____

_____

_____

_____

_____

345. IT'S YOUR BIRTHDAY AND TIME TO BLOW OUT THE CANDLES ON YOUR CAKE. WRITE DOWN YOUR WISH.

347.
IF YOU COULD INVENT A TOOL TO DO A TASK YOU DON'T LIKE, WHAT WOULD IT BE?

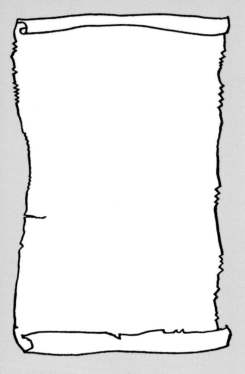

346.
YOU'RE AT THE BEACH AND YOU FIND AN OLD BOTTLE WITH A MESSAGE INSIDE IT. WHAT DOES IT SAY?

348. WHAT IF YOU HAD AN IMAGINARY FRIEND? WHAT WOULD THEY BE LIKE?

349. MAKE UP DEFINITIONS FOR THESE INVENTED WORDS:

SCARIBATED

FIBULOUS

FREEBOLD

VASHY

TENDERNOOSE

350. IF YOU COULD BE A PIXIE OR A GIANT,
WHICH WOULD YOU CHOOSE? WHY?

351. SET A TIMER FOR 30 SECONDS AND JUST WRITE! (IT DOESN'T MATTER WHAT.) STOP WHEN THE TIMER GOES OFF. THIS IS CALLED "FREE WRITING."

352. THINK OF WORDS WITH THE CORRECT NUMBER OF SYLLABLES AND FILL IN THE TABLE BELOW.

ONE-SYLLABLE WORD:	
TWO-SYLLABLE WORD:	
THREE-SYLLABLE WORD:	
FOUR-SYLLABLE WORD:	
FIVE-SYLLABLE WORD:	
SIX-SYLLABLE WORD:	

353.

WRITE DOWN THE FIRST THREE WORDS THAT COME INTO YOUR HEAD WHEN YOU READ THIS WORD: SUNRISE.

354.

THINK OF AN EMOTION TO GO WITH EACH OF THESE COLORS:

GREEN

BLUE

WHITE

YELLOW

PINK

355. CREATE A CHARACTER PROFILE BY FILLING IN THESE DETAILS:

NAME: _____

AGE: _____

WHERE THEY LIVE: _____

WEAKNESS: _____

_____

STRENGTH: _____

_____

ONE PHYSICAL FEATURE: _____

_____

_____

356. PEOPLE USE LANGUAGE DIFFERENTLY WHEN SPEAKING AND WRITING. WHEN SPEAKING, THEY MIGHT USE MORE COLLOQUIAL (INFORMAL) LANGUAGE, OR INCLUDE SLANG. FILL IN THE SPEECH BUBBLES USING INFORMAL LANGUAGE.

357.

IF YOU COULD DESIGN AN AMUSEMENT PARK, WHAT KIND OF PLACE WOULD IT BE? WHAT RIDES OR ATTRACTIONS WOULD IT HAVE?

358. LOOK AT YOUR EYES IN A MIRROR, THEN DESCRIBE THEM HERE.

359. YOU DISCOVER A NEW FLOWER THAT MAKES PEOPLE
GIGGLE WHEN THEY SMELL IT. WHAT DO YOU CALL IT?

360. SCIENTISTS HAVE DISCOVERED A NEW ANIMAL. THEY ARE GOING TO CALL
IT A "TREACLE PONY." WHAT IS IT LIKE? WRITE A DESCRIPTION OF IT.

361. WRITERS USE EMOTIVE LANGUAGE TO MAKE READERS FEEL STRONG EMOTIONS, SUCH AS EXCITEMENT, PITY, OR SHOCK. FOR EXAMPLE, "SHE WAS BUZZING WITH EXCITEMENT; SHE COULDN'T WAIT TO GET TO THE CONCERT." USE EMOTIVE LANGUAGE TO DESCRIBE SOMETHING SAD OR EXCITING YOU HAVE EXPERIENCED.

362. MAKE UP A NEWSPAPER HEADLINE ABOUT ANYTHING YOU LIKE. TRY TO MAKE SURE IT'S ATTENTION GRABBING.

363.

IF YOU COULD HAVE ANY TYPE OF MYTHICAL ANIMAL AS A PET, WHAT WOULD YOU CHOOSE? WHY?

364.

YOU ARE A FAIRY-TALE HERO. YOU HAVE TO FACE THREE "IMPOSSIBLE" TASKS. WHAT ARE THEY?

1._____

_____

_____

2._____

_____

_____

3._____

_____

_____

365.

A WRITER NEEDS TO PERFECT THEIR SIGNATURE SINCE THEY OFTEN SIGN BOOKS FOR THEIR FANS. FINISH THIS BOOK BY SIGNING YOUR NAME TO ALL YOUR WORK!

_____

First American Edition 2021
Kane Miller, A Division of EDC Publishing

Copyright © 2021 Quarto Publishing plc

For information contact:
Kane Miller, A Division of EDC Publishing
PO Box 470663
Tulsa, OK 74147-0663
www.kanemiller.com
www.edcpub.com
www.usbornebooksandmore.com

Library of Congress Control Number: 2020936350

ISBN: 978-1-68464-170-3

Manufactured in Guangdong, China TT102020

1 2 3 4 5 6 7 8 9 10